"Before you open The Book, be sure to spend time in this book. It will enrich and amplify your experience with the Word of God!"

Lee Strobel, author of *The Case for Christ*

"This book will help you read Scripture in a deeper, more meaningful way."

Russell Moore, president, The Ethics & Religious Liberty Commission of the Southern Baptist Convention

"Just as our bodies need right posture for physical health, so our hearts need right posture for spiritual health. Matt Smethurst's book offers a posture for Bible reading that will serve the heart of anyone set on right worship."

Jen Wilkin, Bible teacher and author of *Women of the Word*

"As evidenced by his social media presence, my friend Matt Smethurst is one of the more thoughtful Christian commentators out there today. I'm thankful he's written a book on how to rightly interact with God's Word. This is something that no Christian can afford to neglect."

Shai Linne, Christian hip-hop artist and author of *God Made Me and You*

"This wise guide will help you not only to read God's Word well, but to be transformed by it."

Karen Swallow Prior, professor, Liberty University and author of *On Reading Well*

BEFORE YOU
OPEN *your* BIBLE

NINE HEART POSTURES FOR
APPROACHING GOD'S WORD

MATT SMETHURST

10 Publishing
a division of 10ofthose.com

Copyright © 2019 by Matt Smethurst

First published in Great Britain in 2019 by Matt Smethurst

British Library Cataloguing in Publication Data
A record for this book is available from the British Library

ISBN: 978-1-912373-71-0

Designed by Pete Barnsley (CreativeHoot.com)

Printed in Denmark by Nørhaven

10Publishing, a division of 10ofthose.com
Unit C, Tomlinson Road, Leyland, PR25 2DY, England

Email: info@10ofthose.com
Website: www.10ofthose.com

CONTENTS

v

INTRODUCTION:

TOO DAUNTING OR TOO FAMILIAR?

Have you ever been intimidated by the Bible? It happened to me again thirty minutes ago. I came to a section in my Bible reading plan that has long puzzled me.

This experience isn't uncommon. Few of us are biblical experts—though we may have started enough annual reading plans to be really comfortable with Genesis.

So why does the Bible intimidate us? Sometimes it's because of its *size*. The thing is massive, if you haven't noticed—a whole library wedged between two covers.

Other times we're intimidated by what we *don't* understand. It is an ancient book, after all, filled with names and places and customs and conventions from another cultural world.

Still other times the Bible intimidates us because of what we *do* understand. I think it was Mark Twain who quipped that the parts of the Bible that troubled him most were not the ones he didn't grasp but the ones that he did. It's true; Scripture often doesn't say what we wish it did.

Others, meanwhile, wouldn't say they're necessarily intimidated by their Bibles. A better

> FAMILIARITY CAN BE ONE OF THE MOST DANGEROUS THINGS IN THE WORLD.

word might be *bored*. They believe in it, but they've ceased to be amazed by it because of sheer familiarity.

No matter how valuable or precious they are, it's incredibly easy to take familiar things for granted, isn't it? Familiarity can be one of the most dangerous things in the world.

How we approach things matters in a huge way. The world of sports is an obvious example—and a general analogy for life. Whether we're talking about a pitcher on the mound or a runner at the starting line, an athlete's simple approach can make all the difference.

So whether you are new to the Christian faith or someone who has been following Jesus for a long time, and especially if you are just exploring what Christianity is all about, I hope this book will help open your eyes to all that awaits you in God's Word—and what you may be missing out on simply because of your approach. At the risk of sounding like your mother, the issue could be "poor posture." Of the heart, that is.

Thankfully, there are many good resources on how to read, study, and apply the Bible. But I'm not aware of any that focus exclusively on how to approach it in the first place. This little book aims to do just that. For without the right heart postures, we're not yet ready to start reading.

1

APPROACH YOUR BIBLE

PRAYERFULLY

I might as well begin with a confession: I wasn't planning to include this chapter.

I nearly omitted it for the same reason you're tempted to skim it or skip it.

For most of us, the importance of prayer is not a breaking headline. It's "old news." We are aware that it matters, even if we don't get how it all works. (*If God has planned everything,* you may wonder, *why bother asking him for anything?*) Even if you're not religious at all, you know that followers of Jesus pray. They talk to him—or think that's what they are doing. And if you are a believer, well, is there a topic more basic?

If the Christian faith had a curriculum, the class called "Prayer Matters" wouldn't be an elective for college; it would be a prerequisite for kindergarten.

NEVER ASSUME

Okay, so prayer is foundational. It's really important. But can't we just assume this is true and graduate to the "practical" stuff? Not so fast.

> I AM CONVINCED THAT A PRAYERLESS APPROACH TO GOD'S WORD IS A MAJOR REASON FOR THE LOW-LEVEL DISSATISFACTION THAT HUMS BENEATH THE SURFACE OF OUR LIVES.

The most important things in life should never be glossed over or simply assumed.

I am convinced that a prayerless approach to God's Word is a major reason for the low-level dissatisfaction that hums beneath the surface of our lives. We rob ourselves of joy and peace when we fail to pray. Indeed, approaching Scripture apart from prayer is one of the most counterproductive things we do. For prayerless Christianity is powerless Christianity.

I-O-U-S

You may be familiar with praying in *response* to God's Word, but what does it mean to pray in *anticipation* of it? What does it look like to approach your Bible prayerfully?

It means not rushing into your Bible reading, expecting the pages to magically microwave your cold heart. Now, God is sovereign—which is another way of saying he's *God* and does what he wants (Ps. 115:3). He is more than capable of turning on the microwave even when you haven't asked him. But why not ask him?

Several years ago, I heard John Piper share an acronym that he uses to ready his heart to hear from God. Each letter—I-O-U-S—corresponds to a prayer from the Book of Psalms.[1]

I – "Incline my heart to your testimonies, and not to selfish gain" (Ps. 119:36, ESV)
This is not a flattering request. It assumes our

hearts are bent in the wrong direction, away from what gives life. It's not that we dislike our Bibles; it's just that other things loom larger. Our wish lists seem more enticing, our to-do lists more pressing.

Most mornings, for example, my mind immediately goes to one of three places:

1. What do I have planned for today?

2. What am I going to eat for breakfast?

3. What's happening on social media?

Questions like these are not terrible, but they are telling. They expose the natural bent of my heart. They reveal that while it's effortless to be mindful of self, I have to work to be mindful of God.

Every day I need to be peeled away from my pathetic preoccupation with self. You do too. Thankfully, God loves to de-magnetize our hearts from what is worthless, and re-magnetize them toward what is priceless, all for the sake of our joy. This is where prayer comes in; we just have to ask.

O – "Open my eyes, that I may behold wondrous things out of your law" (Ps. 119:18, ESV)

In many ways, reading the Bible is like reading other books. We ought to approach it the way we'd approach any piece of literature, being sensitive to genre, setting, the author's intent, and all that other good stuff. But there is one

> THE SPIRIT LOVES BRINGING GOD'S WORDS TO LIFE, DAY AFTER DAY, IN THE HEARTS OF THOSE BLINDED BY THE TYRANNY OF WORTHLESS THINGS.

major difference. *The third person of the eternal Trinity breathed out its words.* And the Spirit loves bringing God's words to life, day after day, in the hearts of those blinded by the tyranny of worthless things.

What has captured your imagination? What is enamoring the eyes of your heart? When you open your Bible, don't expect to be put under some mystical spell. Speak directly with the Author. Ask the Spirit to unblind you to the beauty staring you in the face. As Charles

Spurgeon observed, "Texts will often refuse to reveal their treasures till you open them with the key of prayer."[2]

> **WHEN YOU OPEN YOUR BIBLE, DON'T EXPECT TO BE PUT UNDER SOME MYSTICAL SPELL. SPEAK DIRECTLY WITH THE AUTHOR. ASK THE SPIRIT TO UNBLIND YOU TO THE BEAUTY STARING YOU IN THE FACE.**

U – "Unite my heart to fear your name" (Ps. 86:11, ESV)

When I was a boy, my dad once explained why opening the Bible can be such a struggle. "It's almost like Satan's finger is pressing down on the cover," he said. I remember thinking that was weird. Now I believe it's true.

The Bible teaches us that the Devil is crafty. He knows the easiest way to keep us from God's Word is to distract us, to hold up captivating shiny objects, to lure us into thinking about something—*anything*—else.[3]

Perhaps you recognize this scenario: *Okay, Romans chapter 2. Let's do this! Where did I leave off? Okay, this part looks familiar. Man, I love the apostle Paul . . . I am so hungry. Is my lunch meeting tomorrow at 11:30 or 12:30? Let me check . . .*

Amazing, isn't it? Our hearts are fragmented in a thousand different directions. As Piper has written elsewhere, in words that should haunt many of us, "One of the great uses of Twitter and Facebook will be to prove at the Last Day that prayerlessness was not from lack of time."[4]

We must pray earnestly for a *united* heart, lest it drift toward being divided, distracted, and distant from the words of the living God.

S – "Satisfy us in the morning with your steadfast love" (Ps. 90:14, ESV)

It's not just that we're distracted from God, though. We're also dissatisfied in God. Sure, we know he's a significant part of life, but we figure that if we want to be really filled up—really happy—we'll need to look elsewhere.

Sometimes religious people can give the impression that happiness is unspiritual. You can be happy or you can be holy, but surely not both.

Thankfully, the Bible has no patience for this kind of thinking.

Every human being on the planet is seeking happiness. That's not the problem; the problem is that we seek it outside of God. Right quest, wrong destination.

In his 2005 commencement address at Kenyon College, the late American novelist David Foster Wallace captured this universal, even primal, human dynamic. Wallace was not a Christian, and yet his words strike a profound spiritual chord:

> *The compelling reason for maybe choosing some sort of God or spiritual-type thing to worship . . . is that pretty much anything else you worship will eat you alive. If you worship money and things, if they are where you tap real meaning in life, then you will never feel you have enough. Worship your body and beauty and sexual allure and you will always feel ugly. And when time and age start showing, you will die a million deaths before they finally plant you. . . . Worship power, you will end up feeling weak and afraid, and you will need ever more*

power over others to numb you to your own fear.
Worship your intellect, being seen as smart, you
will end up feeling stupid, a fraud, always on
the verge of being found out. But the insidious
thing about these forms of worship is . . . they're
unconscious. They are default settings.[5]

Can you see yourself in the mirror of Wallace's
words? I can. This is why I need to approach
God's Word prayerfully, asking him to satisfy
this restless heart with steadfast love.

2

APPROACH YOUR BIBLE
HUMBLY

When was the last time the Bible astonished you? I don't mean something *in* the Bible. I mean the Bible itself.

Perhaps you're not entirely sure what I'm talking about. The Bible's *existence*? That's always struck you as a given, not a miracle.

I can relate. As a kid, I respected the Bible. I even planned to read it cover to cover one day. But compared to my glossy album of basketball trading cards, it simply lacked luster. *I'll get around to it*, I must've thought while staring at the shelf. *Yawn.*

For years I continued to affirm the truthfulness of Scripture with my lips while functionally neglecting it with my life. Even though I genuinely trusted God and knew much about his Word, I maintained a respectful ambivalence toward it that lasted through high school. It wasn't until my freshman year of college that things decisively changed. (More on that in the next chapter.)

So what was I missing? What did I fail to grasp, or even consider, for so long? *I was missing what the existence of God's Word proves about God himself.*

TALKATIVE GOD

If the existence of the Bible reveals anything about God, it's that he's a talker. He could have remained silent. He really could have. But he didn't. Your Bible is tangible evidence that the Maker of the universe is a communicator; he's someone who initiates, who reveals, who *speaks*.[1]

There are, after all, only two options when it comes to knowledge of our Creator: revelation or speculation. Either he speaks, or we guess.

And he has spoken. As someone once put it, the God of heaven and earth forfeited "his personal privacy" to befriend us.[2] I love that. Your Bible is like an all-access pass into the revealed mind and heart of God.

So far, so good. But here's what I missed growing up. I assumed that since God is a talker, I must somehow deserve his words. Why else would he have bothered to say so much?

DOUBLY UNDESERVING

But not only do I not deserve to hear from God, I am *doubly undeserving* of it. First, because I am simply a created being. Second, because I am a sinner.

It's amazing enough that God would communicate with creatures of the dust. In Genesis 1 and 2, he fashions our first parents and befriends them with words. Again, he didn't have to do this. We run the risk of being so familiar with the story that it somehow fails to stun us, or even to interest us. *Of course God initiated a friendship with Adam and Eve*, we think. *Of course he wanted them to know his love. Of course he talked with them. That's just what God . . . does.*

We should never take for granted that the exalted Creator would befriend the work of his hands. But that's precisely what he did.

As the story continues in Genesis 3, everything unravels as Adam and Eve listen to the whispers

> WE SHOULD NEVER TAKE FOR GRANTED THAT THE EXALTED CREATOR WOULD BEFRIEND THE WORK OF HIS HANDS. BUT THAT'S PRECISELY WHAT HE DID.

of a serpent over the words of God. Eating the fruit wasn't a minor infraction; it was cosmic treason against their good and generous Lord.

Have you ever received the silent treatment after offending someone? It is not pleasant. Sometimes it's deserved; sometimes it's not. Though Adam and Eve deserved the ultimate silent treatment for all eternity, God initiated a conversation. He stooped to speak. He pursued a relationship with rebels, one that would require the death of his only Son to repair.

So, given that we're not only creatures of the dust but traitors against heaven's throne, the talkativeness of God is astounding. He would've been entirely right to leave us to ourselves, sunk in an ocean of ignorance (since we're creatures) and guilt (since we're sinners).

But he didn't. He peeled back the curtain. And then opened his holy mouth.

Any authentic knowledge of God hinges on his generous self-disclosure to us. Only through his words can we discover who he is, what he's like, what he's after, and how we can know him.

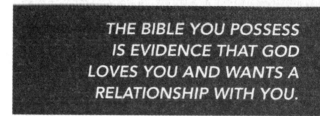

THE BIBLE YOU POSSESS IS EVIDENCE THAT GOD LOVES YOU AND WANTS A RELATIONSHIP WITH YOU.

This ought to humble us deeply. The Bible you possess is evidence that God loves you and wants a relationship with you. No matter who you are or how many times you've spurned his love, he is still moving toward you, still talking to you—still befriending you—through a book.

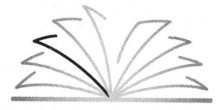

3

APPROACH YOUR BIBLE
DESPERATELY

My first college roommate, let's call him Michael, was a stranger when we met on move-in day. So I breathed a sigh of relief as we quickly hit it off. Ah, sweet relational bliss. Future groomsman material?

It lasted 48 hours.

Michael wasn't my biggest fan. Okay, that's an understatement. Michael hated me. What he loved was dispatching naughty words to remind me of that fact.

The cruelty began the moment I left to attend my first campus ministry meeting. Michael made it clear he had no patience for Christians like me. The more involved in campus fellowship I became, the more he seemed to resent me.

Though I can now look back on this situation and smile, at the time it was the hardest thing I'd ever faced. To this day I'm not sure I have ever tried to love someone with more intentionality than I tried to love Michael that first semester. But the harder I tried, the worse it became.

I wasn't just perplexed; I was devastated. Here I was in college, trying to live for God, and I wasn't even welcome in my own room.

SURVIVAL FOOD

In order to survive the situation with Michael, I started reading my Bible. Devouring it, really. Perhaps the language of survival sounds a bit dramatic to you, but that's what it felt like to my eighteen-year-old self. I realized I couldn't survive a single day with Michael if I didn't begin the day with God. I wasn't approaching my Bible out of duty. I wasn't even approaching it out of delight. I was approaching it out of desperation.

The Lord changed my life that year. He used a painful relationship to drive me to his Word, and I fell in love with him through its pages.

NOT AN ACCESSORY

In Jeremiah 15:16, the prophet addresses God with startling language: "When your words came, I ate them; they were my joy and my heart's delight, for I bear your name, LORD God Almighty."

If you read the Bible, you'll never get the impression that it's meant to be a mere hobby in your life. It's meant to be your food.

Perhaps you're familiar with Jesus's famous words when being tempted by Satan in the wilderness: "It is written, 'Man shall not live on bread alone, but on every word that comes from the mouth of God'" (Matt. 4:4; cf. Deut. 8:3).

STOP EATING CHEESE PUFFS

Have you ever ruined your appetite for an epic dinner by snacking all day? It's terrible. You wish you could work up an appetite, but it's too late. The steak is on the table and you're not hungry.

This is how we often treat God's Word, if we're honest. Is it any wonder that nibbling long enough from the table of the world would leave us with little appetite left for God?[1] If we're snacking on cheese puffs, we shouldn't be surprised when we don't have room for steak.

> IS IT ANY WONDER THAT NIBBLING LONG ENOUGH FROM THE TABLE OF THE WORLD WOULD LEAVE US WITH LITTLE APPETITE LEFT FOR GOD? IF WE'RE SNACKING ON CHEESE PUFFS, WE SHOULDN'T BE SURPRISED WHEN WE DON'T HAVE ROOM FOR STEAK.

Consider three diagnostic questions, worth asking yourself on a regular basis:

1. Do I approach the Bible more like it's a snack or like it's a feast?

2. Is it more accurate to say I'm *willing* to hear from God or that I'm *desperate* to hear from him?

3. Am I merely *interested* in the Scriptures or am I also *internalizing* them?

There are so many days I don't feel desperate to hear God's voice. I tell myself the Bible's a feast, but it sure feels like finger food. I know I should have an appetite, but I don't. I like cheese puffs.

Perhaps you can relate? If you struggle to approach God's Word desperately, I have a challenge for you. Find a Christian friend and slowly work through Psalm 119 together. It may take a few meetings—the psalm is longer than twenty-six books of the Bible! But it's like smelling salts for the soul. Here's a taste:

> My soul is consumed with longing for your laws
> at all times. . . . I hold fast to your statutes. . . .
> I open my mouth and pant, longing for your
> commands (Ps. 119:20, 31, 131).

Don't you want to feel like that? Don't you want to ache for the words of life? Don't you want to get rid of the snack bags on the floor of your car and walk into the restaurant for a four-course dinner? God himself is the chef and the host, and there's a seat with your name on it. Come in.

Shortly before his death, after rehearsing God's law one final time, Moses looks at the

> GOD HIMSELF IS THE CHEF AND THE HOST, AND THERE'S A SEAT WITH YOUR NAME ON IT. COME IN.

people of Israel and says, "These are not just idle words for you—they are your life" (Deut. 32:47). The stakes could not be higher.

Your soul will wither and die without your Bible. Approach it desperately.

4

APPROACH YOUR BIBLE
STUDIOUSLY

Do you consider yourself a theologian? I assume not. I certainly didn't for many years.

Looking back, however, it's clear I didn't understand what theology was about. I basically figured it was a holy hobby for Christian geeks. Sure, I was vaguely thankful for scholars who stroked their chins and wrote Bible commentaries, but my working assumption was that the *real* action in the Christian life was with the heart and the hands.

When I was a sophomore or junior in college, however, I came across a verse in the Book of Psalms that I'd never noticed before: "Great are the works of the LORD, studied by all who delight in them" (Ps. 111:2, ESV).

I was a bit startled. "Studied" is not the verb I would've expected. "Acknowledged" or "remembered" or "celebrated," maybe, but

> **APPARENTLY, WHEN IT COMES TO CHRISTIANITY, CLASS IS ALWAYS IN SESSION.**

"studied"? I thought Christianity was supposed to be fun. Why is the Bible talking like it's finals week? But if God's Word is filled with his works, I must have much to learn.

Apparently, when it comes to Christianity, class is always in session.

STUDY FROM LOVE

Think about it: We study what we love, don't we?

When I was a kid, I studied Michael Jordan statistics—not because I loved numbers (I actually hated math), but because I loved Jordan. It's a silly example, but it reveals a timeless truth: We long to learn about what we love. I didn't study Jordan stats because I liked studying. I didn't study Jordan stats under coercion. I studied Jordan stats because I wanted to learn as much as I possibly could about the hero I revered.

On the other hand, imagine you asked me about my wife. I could respond, with tears in my eyes, "Oh, she's incredible—the most amazing girl I've ever known! She's from Oregon, has gorgeous red hair, and hates chocolate." My actual chocolate-loving brunette wife who hails from Virginia would not exactly be honored by this description, now, would she? Of course not. I can gush all day long about what my wife is like, but unless my words reflect who she actually is, she'll be insulted.

If we're so careful to study and accurately represent our heroes and lovers, why are we lackadaisical in how we talk about our Creator?

THINK IT OUT

As we have seen, the Old Testament psalms challenge us to adopt a posture of careful study as we approach God's Word. This theme continues in the New Testament. In Matthew 22, a Pharisee comes to Jesus with a question:

> *"Teacher, which is the greatest commandment in the Law?" Jesus replied, "Love the Lord your God with all your heart and with all your soul and with all your mind" (Matt. 22:36–37).*

Many of us know this verse and love the heart-and-soul part. But we shouldn't stop too soon. The greatest commandment, Jesus insists, includes loving God with your mind.

How are you doing in that department? Do you approach your Bible with an alert and engaged mind? Are you prepared to read slowly, to ponder carefully, and to study seriously?

In Acts 17, Paul and Silas have fled persecution in Thessalonica and have arrived in Berea, a city in northern Greece. They enter the local Jewish synagogue and begin proclaiming that Jesus is the Messiah. How does the audience respond?

> *Now the Berean Jews were of more noble character than those in Thessalonica, for they*

received the message with great eagerness and
examined the Scriptures every day to see if
what Paul said was true (Acts 17:11).

The Berean Jews don't listen mindlessly;
they check the teaching against the Hebrew
Scriptures. Notice Luke doesn't rebuke them for
not taking an apostle at his word; he *commends*
them. The Bereans' impulse to pause and slow
down—to study—reveals their noble character.
They are loving God with their minds.

STUDY TO WORSHIP

Romans 9–11 are three of the weightiest
chapters in the entire Bible—the deep end
of the theological pool. And yet notice how
Paul concludes:

Oh, the depth of the riches of the wisdom
and knowledge of God! How unsearchable his
judgments, and his paths beyond tracing out!
. . . For from him and through him and for him
are all things. To him be glory forever. Amen
(Rom. 11:33, 36).

So, what arrested Paul's heart and moved him to erupt in worship? In the context of the passage, the answer is plain: doctrine. Doctrine drove him to delight. His theology exploded like fireworks into doxology.[1]

We study God to praise God. And we cannot praise what we do not know. Friend, don't let anyone ever convince you that theology is impractical, that it distracts, that it impedes worship or hinders mission. Any good thing can be misused, of course, but the purpose of theology has never been to make you feel smarter. It's certainly not to make you feel

> THE PURPOSE OF THEOLOGY IS TO STOKE YOUR WORSHIP, TO DEEPEN YOUR LOVE, TO FUEL YOUR MISSION, AND TO SUSTAIN YOUR LIFE.

superior. The purpose of theology is to stoke your worship, to deepen your love, to fuel your mission, and to sustain your life.

When suffering arrives unbidden in your life, and the bottom falls out, you will either have something solid and sure to stand on—or not.

YOU'RE A THEOLOGIAN, SO BECOME A GOOD ONE

In one sense, all it takes to be a theologian is to have an opinion about God. That's it. The moment you think or say anything about him or her or it or whatever "God" is to you, you're doing theology.

The real question, therefore, is not whether you are a theologian. It's whether you are a good one.

Do you want deeper worship? Richer joy? Strength for today and bright hope for tomorrow, as the hymn says? Then approach your Bible with a learner's posture, asking the Author to teach you marvelous things. Don't just waterski across the surface of Scripture's waters. Put on scuba gear. Dive in and explore the wonders of the biblical world. Some fine resources to aid you in this immersive, exhilarating journey are listed at the back of this book.

As my campus minister, Dan Flynn, used to say, "The Bible is the best book that's ever read me." Master it. Better yet, submerge yourself in it, and let it master you.

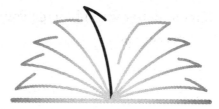

5

APPROACH YOUR BIBLE
OBEDIENTLY

"Obedience" is not one of my favorite words (except when I'm with my kids). It doesn't give me all the feels; it doesn't make me warm inside. In fact, the concept seems rather cold. There's an almost robotic quality to it.

Maybe that's just me, though. Maybe you have the word framed on your wall, or Instagrammed over a nice filter, or even tattooed on your ankle. In Hebrew, of course.

Throughout our lives we're being told to obey. Obey your parents. Obey your teacher.

Obey your coach. Obey your professors. Obey your landlord. Obey your governing authorities. Obey your doctors.

Obey, obey, obey. I doubt anyone reading this book is on a quest to find another person or institution to whom they should submit.

Exactly, you may be thinking. *So why would I want to obey the Bible? I've seen one; it's thick enough with rules to make a great doorstop. And I hear the author is quite demanding. I have plenty of obligations already, thank you.*[1]

CUSTOM DESIGNED

I used to live in a foreign country, and, despite attending class each day, I never mastered the language. I was functional but not fluent. As you can imagine, this made it tricky when trying to share the gospel story with the friends I'd made. Illustrations had to be really simple. For example, I would often say something to this effect:

> *Fish are made for the water, and birds for the air, right? Now imagine a fish who decides he's tired of being restricted to the water. He wants to be free, to experience the joy of life on land. So*

he manages to flop around and "free" himself onto dry ground—which turns out to be a death sentence. Why? He was only designed for water, not for air. Conversely, imagine a seagull growing jealous of the freedom he witnesses in the ocean below. I'm sick of being confined to the air, he thinks. I want to be truly free. So he plunges in and perishes. Why? He was only designed for air, not for water.

In a similar way, just as the fish was built for water and the bird for air, so you were built for God—and you will not find true life and freedom anywhere else.[2]

It's an elementary metaphor, I know. But it's also a mirror. We are more like these disgruntled creatures than we may care to admit. The distance between their logic and ours can be uncomfortably thin.

Biblical obedience is not about keeping an arbitrary set of rules; it's about living in accordance with our design, in harmony with our Maker. Because he wants us to flourish, he restricts us in order to truly free us. He prohibits us to drive us to what is good. He lays boundaries with hands of love.

GOOD FOR YOU

To the degree that we approach Scripture prayerfully and studiously, we will be positioned to catch easy-to-miss phrases. Hear, for example, the words of Moses:

> And now, Israel, what does the LORD your God ask of you but to fear the LORD your God, to walk in obedience to him, to love him, to serve the LORD your God with all your heart and with all your soul, and to observe the LORD's commands and decrees that I am giving you today for your own good? (Deut. 10:12–13).

Did you catch those rapid-fire requirements? There are five: *fear*, *walk*, *serve*, *obey*, and the central one, *love*. They function like links in a chain, or like distinct notes of obedience in the music of your life. Moses's call is comprehensive; God is interested in both your actions and your attitude. Feet, hands, mind, heart—he wants it all.

Rather daunting, huh?

But here's the part we're inclined to miss entirely: "for your own good." Did you catch those four words when you read the passage? They revolutionize it.

So why is God making all-encompassing claims on your life today, even as you read this

> YOU WERE MADE FOR OBEDIENCE, LIKE FISH FOR WATER AND BIRDS FOR AIR.

book? It is because he deserves your obedience. But it is also because you were made for obedience, like fish for water and birds for air.

This news is not always easy to swallow, but it's good: The One who flung the stars into space and spoke galaxies into being is far too qualified to govern just one or two small provinces in your life. He loves you too much to leave you in charge of an existence you didn't design. Just as there are physical laws like gravity built into creation, there are moral laws you were born to honor. A disobedient believer makes no more sense than a disenchanted bird trying to reach the ocean floor. In infinite wisdom and goodness, God has structured his moral universe in a particular way. We can trust him. If we refuse, we won't just be breaking his laws; we'll be breaking *ourselves* against them.

NOTE OF URGENCY

"Slow obedience is no obedience," we tell our kids. A similar note of urgency rings through the pages of the New Testament.

Consider the words of Jesus in the Sermon on the Mount:

> *Therefore everyone who hears these words of mine and puts them into practice is like a wise man who built his house on the rock. The rain came down, the streams rose, and the winds blew and beat against that house; yet it did not fall, because it had its foundation on the rock. But everyone who hears these words of mine and does not put them into practice is like a foolish man who built his house on sand. The rain came down, the streams rose, and the winds blew and beat*

against that house, and it fell with a great crash (Matt. 7:24–27, emphasis mine).

And James:

Do not merely listen to the word, and so deceive yourselves. Do what it says (Jas. 1:22).

And also John:

Whoever says "I know him," but does not do what he commands is a liar, and the truth is not in that person (1 John 2:4–5).

And on and on. In fact, let's return to Jesus for a moment. Shortly before his ascension and enthronement, he delivers marching orders to his disciples. We know it as the Great Commission:

Jesus came to them and said, "All authority in heaven and on earth has been given to me. Therefore go and make disciples of all nations, baptizing them in the name of the Father and of the Son and of the Holy Spirit, and teaching them to obey everything I have commanded

> you. *And surely I am with you always, to the*
> *very end of the age" (Matt. 28:18–20).*

When we think about this famous charge, we often focus on themes like evangelism, discipleship, and missions. As we should. But again, it's vital to read slowly and studiously, lest we miss easy-to-overlook words.

Jesus does not merely say, "Teach them everything I have commanded you." That would be a simple call for information transfer. Instead he says, "Teach them to obey everything I have commanded you." The risen King sends his servants into the world not merely to impart information, but to promote obedience. Have you ever thought about the fact that *holiness* is part of the Great Commission? This means that no matter how many disciples you are making or how jazzed up about missions you feel, if you are not pursuing obedience, then the Great Commission remains unfulfilled in your life.

UNEXPECTED PATH

Maybe you're still skeptical. Following a demanding God still seems like a drag. Again, I want to reiterate that the Bible is not an arbitrary list of prohibitions; it's an epic story of a Creator more committed to your joy than you could imagine. Entrusting each sphere of your life to him, therefore, is not something you do instead of enjoying him; it's the way you enjoy him. Following him is not an alternative to your joy; it's the secret to it.

So approach your Bible obediently, because obedience produces joy. Which leads us to the next chapter.

6

APPROACH YOUR BIBLE
JOYFULLY

As a dad, I'm not always pleased when my kids obey me.

This is because they need to obey with a glad and sincere heart, and that is not always the case. Any child can muster grudging compliance. I'm longing to see a willing spirit and joyful trust.

The command to be joyful permeates the Scriptures, but it's a bit strange if you think about it. Joy is an emotion, not a behavior. How can I be *told* to feel a certain way? What if I want to but just . . . don't?

Let's start with something we don't often think about when it comes to God.

DEEP DELIGHTS

It may sound somewhat strange, but God is happy. Happier than the happiest person you've ever known. His gladness stretches back before the beginning, when infinite joy was contained within a triangle of love. For all of eternity, Father, Son, and Holy Spirit—one God in three persons—delighted to share the joy of divinity with one another.[1]

So why did the triune God create the universe? Was he lacking something, perhaps compliant creatures to complete him? No. The creation of the world was an explosion of joy—not a filling up, but a spilling out. Consider that for a moment: Not only the astounding natural world, but you and I, created by God, are an overflow of his exceeding joy. In extravagant generosity, the persons of the Trinity decided to share their boundless gladness with the work of their hands.[2]

You may wonder what this mini theology lesson has to do with approaching your Bible joyfully. Everything—because *that's* the God who exhaled its words, and in whose image you are made.

You were made to be happy in a happy God.

NOT AN ACCESSORY

Tragically, of course, the "happily ever after" of Genesis 1–2 was short-lived. Now we inhabit a Genesis 3 world, riddled with darkness and dysfunction and death, as I'm sure you've experienced. (If you haven't, keep living.)

Have you ever wondered why the Bible is so long? One reason is because God is so patient. It's the long story of his longsuffering. And why has he been so patient? Because he loves us, yes. But even more specifically, because he's been carefully executing a plan—a plan to share his endless joy with his rescued people, a multitude no one can count (Rev. 7:9).[3]

According to the Bible, joy is not an accessory to the Christian life, a perk for shiny saints who can turn their frowns upside down. Rather, joy is tenacious. It fights. It grips the promises of God and won't let go. And joy is not a mere good mood; it is ballast in our boats, an anchor in our storms, an immovable rock to stand on when the waves of life threaten to flatten us.

Far from being a peripheral subtheme in Scripture, joy is the heartbeat of God. No wonder it is at the core of his ultimate story and is intended to shape our smaller stories, too. Consider a snapshot of its centrality:

- What is the gospel? It is "good news that will cause great joy" (Luke 2:10).

- What is death? "Come and share your master's happiness!" (Matt. 25:21).

- What is the goal of prayer? "Ask and you will receive, and your joy will be complete" (John 16:24).

- What is the goal of fellowship? "I hope to visit you and talk with you face to face, so that our joy may be complete" (2 John 12).

And what's the goal of engaging with Scripture? In chapter three we looked at Jeremiah 15:16 and focused on the first half of the verse. Now see what results from the prophet's dinner: "When your words came, I ate them; they were my joy and my heart's delight" (Jer. 15:16).

Gladness of heart, Jeremiah discovered, is downstream from the feast. The same is true today. Despite what our culture tells you, real joy is not found in listening to yourself; it's found in listening intently to God. It's found when your "delight is in the law of the LORD" (Ps. 1:2); when

> DESPITE WHAT OUR CULTURE TELLS YOU, REAL JOY IS NOT FOUND IN LISTENING TO YOURSELF; IT'S FOUND IN LISTENING INTENTLY TO GOD.

your happiness is tethered not to circumstances but to promises; when you can't get enough of your Bible.

The New Testament only advances this theme. Here's how Jesus puts it to his disciples:

> *These things I have spoken to you, that my joy may be in you, and that your joy may be full (John 15:11, ESV).*

And here's what he prays to his Father:

> . . . *now I am coming to you, and these things I*
> *speak in the world, that they may have my joy*
> *fulfilled in themselves (John 17:13, ESV).*

Observe also the words of John:

> . . . *we are writing these things so that our joy*
> *may be complete (1 John 1:4, ESV).*

Did you hear the refrain? These things, these things, these things—namely, words. Some spoken (by Jesus), some written (by John), but all the breath of God, and all preserved for us in his Word.

The purpose of the words of Jesus and his apostles—the purpose of your Bible, friend—is to flood your heart with joy.

WHEN DELIGHT DRIES UP

I already mentioned that biblical joy is not the same thing as being chipper or maintaining a glass-half-full temperament. Hell is filled with former glass-half-full people. Real joy is so much more, and so much better.

One last thing, though, lest you get the impression that Bible reading is an uninterrupted joyfest for me. It's not. Cracking open God's Word often feels like a duty, not a delight. It requires discipline. It will for you, too. But as with so much in life—eating healthy, working out, and other wise things I struggle to do—it

> **IT IS THE NATURE OF DISCIPLINE TO GIVE WAY TO DELIGHT.**

is the nature of discipline to give way to delight. Not every time, and not all at once. But steadily and increasingly, until the day we see our King face to face and behold him in his beauty—with joy that never ends (Isa. 33:17; 1 Cor. 13:12).

7

APPROACH YOUR BIBLE
EXPECTANTLY

Are you a good waiter? I'm not talking about restaurants; I mean are you usually good at waiting for things to happen?

For many of us the answer is *no*, but for different reasons. Some of us aren't good at waiting because we're so excited. We're optimistic, chomping at the bit for that sparkling thing—a vacation, an album release, a graduation day, a wedding day, and so on. We can be so eager about the future that we fail to embrace the present. Others of us, meanwhile, aren't good at waiting for a very different reason: we're sick of it. We've been waiting forever. Yet no matter how often we've prayed or how hard we've tried, we're still stuck, still here, still spinning our wheels. The job, the spouse, the child, the "big break" we're hoping for—will it ever happen? Doesn't seem so.[1]

If younger people tend to fall into the first bad-waiter category, older folks are more prone to fall into the second. No matter how old we are or what life has thrown our way, we all have a relationship with expectations. And . . . it's complicated.

Expectations—now there's a strong word. It almost has a ring of certainty to it. And yet so many of us aren't naïve; we know better than to expect much from anyone or anything in this life. Can you blame us? We've been let down too many times.

UNPARALLELED POWER

The Bible, however, defies human expectations. Whether we're eager optimists or seasoned pessimists, the Word of God doesn't fit into our neat categories. It has a way of challenging our assumptions and shattering our classifications. No cliché can describe it; no opposition can stop it; no doubt can weaken it.

Friend, no matter how much life has let you down, God's Word never will. It can bear the weight of your expectations. It is unlike anything else you own. For since its ultimate author is God, it is a book of unparalleled power.

On October 31, 2017, Christians worldwide celebrated the 500th anniversary of the launch of the Protestant Reformation. Among other things, the Reformation was a recovery of the Scriptures and the gospel that lit up Europe. One of the best statements from the era was something Martin Luther said as he reflected on the miracle of what had taken place through and around him, despite intense opposition from a corrupt Catholic Church at the time:

I opposed indulgences and all the papists, but never with force. I simply taught, preached, and wrote God's Word; otherwise I did nothing. And while I slept, or drank Wittenberg beer with my friends Philip and Amsdorf, the Word so greatly weakened the papacy that no prince

*or emperor ever inflicted such losses upon it. I
did nothing; the Word did everything.*[2]

Everything, Luther said, because God's glory is in
a category by itself and is shared with no other
(Isa. 42:8).

FACEPALM

When I lived overseas, I got to know a college
student named "James." We'd met playing
basketball and had become fast friends. But, just
like virtually everyone around him, he had never
heard about Jesus Christ.

Over the course of several weeks, I shared
the gospel with him a few times. He seemed
interested, and asked great questions, but he
couldn't disavow the atheistic worldview that
had been ingrained in him for his entire life.

One day, I secured a copy of a film about Jesus
in James's language, and we scheduled a time
to watch it together. I had never seen it before
and didn't know what to expect. But given all
the positive stories and statistics associated
with the movie, I was eager for James to see it.
I remember it was my last day of ministry for

the semester—the winter holiday was about to begin, and my parents were arriving for a visit the following day. I was in a great mood. And when James and I sat down in my apartment living room and I inserted the DVD, my hopes were high.

I'm not sure if James heard a noise about seven minutes into the film, but if he did, it was my hopes being dashed on the floor. You see, James was a hip and modern college dude who had seen far more of Hollywood's latest offerings than I had. The film, meanwhile, was on the cutting edge of 1979. Sure, the script was a verbatim presentation of Luke's Gospel, but I felt embarrassed to be subjecting James to what I saw as subpar acting and cringeworthy cinematography—*Is that Jesus levitating?*—for two long hours. Honestly, I feared it would have a counterproductive effect, making Christianity look sillier to him than it did before. I was mortified and regretted showing him the film.

When the film ended and the credits rolled, I braced for his verdict. James turned and looked at me and, with sincerity in his eyes, simply said: "That was the best movie I have ever seen." I was shocked. That afternoon, James placed his faith in Jesus Christ.

LESSON LEARNED

This story doesn't just convict me of my often pathetic lack of faith; it inspires me to keep leaning on the Holy Spirit and the power of his Word—not human ingenuity or "wisdom"—to do the impossible. Hear Paul's words to the church at Corinth:

> For the message of the cross is foolishness to those who are perishing, but to us who are being saved it is the power of God. . . . Has not God made foolish the wisdom of the world? For since in the wisdom of God the world through its wisdom did not know him, God was pleased through the foolishness of what was preached to save those who believe. Jews demand signs and Greeks look for wisdom, but we preach Christ crucified: a stumbling block to Jews and foolishness to Gentiles, but to those whom God has called, both Jews and Greeks, Christ the power of God and the wisdom of God. For the foolishness of God is wiser than human wisdom, and the weakness

of God is stronger than human strength (1 Cor. 1:18, 20–25).

I am so grateful that the gospel message is not a rough draft, or a weak crutch, or an irrelevant historical relic, but God's explosive power to save

> WE CAN SCHEDULE MEETINGS, BUT PRAISE GOD THAT HE SCHEDULES CONVERSIONS.

anyone—like James, or like you—who trusts in Christ alone (Rom. 1:16).

That afternoon with James, I needed to relearn a simple and yet easily forgettable lesson: We can schedule meetings, but praise God that he schedules conversions.

CHANGE AGENT

We don't only have reason to trust the Bible's power to save, however. We can also trust its power to overhaul our lives and carry us securely through the ups and downs of life.

In fact, Jesus prays this for his future followers: "Sanctify them by your truth; your word is truth" (John 17:17). What an interesting request. Jesus is effectively asking, *Father, sanctify them— consecrate them, change them, conform them to my image—by your Word.* In other words, *Transform them through their Bibles.*

And Jesus means *all* parts of the Bible. Did you know even books like Leviticus—where Bible reading plans crash and burn—were written to encourage and strengthen you? Listen to these words of Paul:

> *For everything that was written in the past was written to teach us, so that through the endurance taught in the Scriptures and the encouragement they provide we might have hope (Rom. 15:4).*

Again, note the use of the word *everything*. Paul is declaring that the entirety of the Scriptures, including the Old Testament, is for you—to instruct you, to encourage you, to help you endure, and to steel your heart with hope.

So when you come to your Bible, come with anticipation. I assure you that among its pages you'll discover everything you need, and more than you expect.

8

APPROACH YOUR BIBLE
COMMUNALLY

For many years I loved Jesus, loved the Scriptures, loved theology, affirmed the importance of community, and yet still basically approached my Christianity as a solo sport. Now, I never thought, *I love Jesus but not the church*. It was more subtle than that, more like, *I love Jesus but don't really need the church*. If my Christian life was a meal, the church was just a side dish: a nice addition but entirely optional.

I wish someone had gently pointed me to the Bible I loved and shown me the breathtaking vision it casts for the Christian life—and how stunted mine was by comparison. (I'm sure people did, actually, but I was just too blind, or unwilling, to see it.)

Christianity is not a solo sport, thankfully. It is a community project, a team effort.

WISDOM IS COLLECTIVE

None of us opens God's Word in a vacuum. We are complex individuals who all come to our Bibles with luggage carts of experiences

> *WE ARE COMPLEX INDIVIDUALS WHO COME TO OUR BIBLES WITH LUGGAGE CARTS OF EXPERIENCES AND INTUITIONS, BELIEFS AND BIASES.*

and intuitions, beliefs and biases. There is no such thing as a "neutral" reading of any book— especially one that makes all-encompassing claims over our lives.

In addition, we are all wired differently. While some are inclined to read the Bible more academically, others are apt to read it more devotionally (though, to clarify, these aren't mutually exclusive; they should go together). In the world of sports, we sometimes hear of a particular athlete who is the "complete package." *She can do it all*, people say. When it comes to understanding and applying Scripture, however, no one lives up to that description. It's imperative, therefore, that we approach Scripture alongside others, in the context of a diverse community—otherwise our experiences will limit us, our preferences will govern us, and our biases will blind us.[1]

It is so easy to impose our pet agendas on God's Word without realizing it. For example, I might read it only in light of some personal situation I have experienced or look for it to confirm my previously held positions.[2] We desperately need other Christians— ideally those who are different from us—to function in our lives as both barrier-setters and barrier-removers, simultaneously keeping us from reading wrongly and freeing us to read wisely.[3]

WORD-FILLED FRIENDSHIPS

The earliest Christians didn't waste any time in rallying together around God's Word. Luke summarizes the rhythm of their lives: "They devoted themselves to the apostles' teaching and to fellowship, to the breaking of bread and to prayer" (Acts 2:42). In today's highly individualistic society, it's so easy to try to devote yourself to the apostles' teaching—that is, to Scripture—apart from any meaningful fellowship. Of course it's very important to regularly read your Bible alone. But the early church set an example that is crucial for us to apply: fellowship with others anchored in God's Word and prayer. In fact, this is precisely what Paul tells the Colossians:

> Let the message of Christ dwell among you richly as you teach and admonish one another with all wisdom through psalms, hymns, and songs from the Spirit, singing to God with gratitude in your hearts (Col. 3:16).

It's a bit unfortunate that our English Bibles don't say "y'all," since the word "you" in Scripture is pluralized the vast majority of the time. One typical example is this challenge to all those in the Colossian church to "let the word of Christ dwell in *you* richly," which presumes the members aren't a bunch of spiritual silos. They're doing life together, as a body.

Did you know that even Peter—rock of the church and apostle of the risen Christ—needed someone else to correct him (Gal. 2:11–21)? If Peter wasn't above making serious mistakes, we're not either.

Or consider Apollos, whom Luke describes as "a learned man, with a thorough knowledge of the Scriptures" (Acts 18:24). He knew and taught his Bible well. And yet even he needed two others, Priscilla and Aquila, who took him aside and "explained to him the way of God more adequately" (Acts 18:26). Again, if Apollos wasn't above misreading God's Word, neither are we.

PASTORS ARE GIFTS

While godly peers in your life are an important means of Christian growth, be sure to recognize your crucial need for godly pastors, as well. Spirituals leaders are gifts from God for your spiritual good (see Eph. 4:11–14). God's design for the church includes pastors and elders who are meant, among other things, to help you better understand and apply the Word of God.[4] If you belong to a church where that's not happening, find a new one. Pastor and author Thabiti Anyabwile puts it pointedly: "If you don't need your Bible at church, then the Bible says you don't need that church."[5]

Pastors are also charged by God to help protect you from all sorts of heresy, damaging doctrine, and any corruption to the pure gospel. Among the qualifications for an elder, Paul writes: "He must hold firmly to the trustworthy message as it has been taught, so that he can encourage others by sound doctrine and refute those who oppose it" (Titus 1:9).

So, friend, prioritize finding a healthy, Bible-saturated, gospel-centered church.[6] And once you find it, join it. Commit. Submit your life to the oversight of its leaders and to the care and accountability of its members. God loves you deeply, and this is the pattern he set in motion with the early church to enhance your spiritual well-being.

PHONE A FRIEND

Some of the richest, most profitable times of Bible reading in my life occurred while sitting across the table from my friend Dave. Every Thursday night in college, after our campus ministry meeting, we would go to the local IHOP restaurant and study books of the Bible together. At this moment, I'm looking at an old Bible with notes and coffee stains from those times. We journeyed phrase by phrase through Genesis and Proverbs, Hebrews and John. (Song of Solomon would have been awkward.) Dave and I experienced

> *DON'T LET THIS WEEK GO BY WITHOUT INVITING ANOTHER BELIEVER TO MEET WITH YOU REGULARLY TO READ GOD'S WORD.*

the joy of discovery, savoring words that spoke to each of us individually and both of us together.

So here's my challenge for you: No matter what your schedule is like or what stage of life you're in, don't let this week go by without inviting another believer to meet with you regularly to read God's Word. That's it—nothing fancy. I can promise you it'll be a recurring feast. Just remember to lay off the cheese puffs.

9

APPROACH YOUR BIBLE

CHRISTO-CENTRICALLY

Okay, "Christocentrically" is a pretty big word. But you'll see what I mean.

This is not yet a Christian book. I mean, in a sense it is—I've quoted Jesus and the New Testament plenty of times. But *much* of what I've written could very well be affirmed by someone who rejects Jesus as the Messiah. A devout Jew, for example, could seek to approach the Hebrew Scriptures prayerfully, humbly, desperately, studiously, obediently, joyfully, expectantly, and communally.

So we can't finish yet—not without the most important chapter. This chapter isn't the most important because it's the best written, or because it's the most interesting or engaging. Nor is it the most important simply because it's the grand finale, the *denouement*. It's the most important because it zeroes in on what your Bible is ultimately about.

Miss this, and you miss it all.

FLOATING ZOOS AND DUSTY DRAWERS

If you grew up in church, you're probably familiar with all the well-known Bible stories. You've marveled at Noah's floating zoo, you've faced down giants in your life like David, maybe you've even dared to be a Daniel. And that's just the Old Testament. In the Gospels you learned about Jesus's miracles, which were pretty cool, and you also probably learned that these stories aren't just intended to amaze; they're meant to make you a better person. See how generous that little boy was with his lunch? Go and do likewise.

If you didn't grow up in church and aren't as familiar with the Bible, you may assume that the Bible is a well-meaning series of morality tales, or an anthology of philosophical musings, or an archaic rulebook that ought to remain confined to hotel-room drawers. Indeed, increasing numbers of people today believe that Scripture is downright dangerous, a tool to oppress the weak and prevent the gullible from being true to themselves.

Churchgoer or not, if you resonate even slightly with any of these sentiments, I am so glad that you are still reading this book—because I have some great news for you.

TIME TO REIMAGINE

Contrary to popular belief, Scripture is not simply a collection of ethical principles, moral platitudes, or abstract life lessons. Imagine a single, unfolding, thrilling drama; a story of epic proportions that is more fascinating than your favorite fairy tale, because it is true. That's God's Word.

If we ever hope to properly handle the stories *in* the Bible, we must first grasp the story *of* the Bible. And that story, the one that traverses its way from Genesis to Revelation, though recorded *for* you, is not finally *about* you. The focus is far higher and the hero far better. Given the Bible's astounding diversity, the plotline's fundamental coherence is striking:

- 66 books of various genres
- 40 plus authors from a variety of backgrounds and occupations
- 1,500 plus years
- 10 civilizations
- 3 continents
- 3 languages
- 1 unified story of redemption

The Bible has one ultimate plan, one ultimate plot, one ultimate champion, one ultimate King. This is what "Christocentrically" means—centered on Christ.

In Luke 24, shortly after his resurrection, Jesus appears incognito to two of his followers on a road. Bewildered and breathless, they relay the buzz surrounding the inexplicably empty tomb. It's the *inexplicably* part that prompts Jesus, still unrecognized, to speak:

> He said to them, "How foolish you are, and how slow to believe all that the prophets have spoken! Did not the Messiah have to suffer these things and then enter his glory?" And beginning with Moses and all the Prophets, he explained to them what was said in all the Scriptures concerning himself (Luke 24:25–27).

After revealing himself to his eleven disciples shortly thereafter, Jesus reiterates the same point:

> He said to them, "This is what I told you while I was still with you: Everything must be fulfilled that is written about me in the Law of Moses, the Prophets and the Psalms." Then he opened their minds so they could understand the Scriptures (Luke 24:44–45).

It wasn't only *after* his resurrection that Jesus spoke this way, however. For example, before

his death he had explained to the Pharisees—
the Jewish religious establishment, the "Bible
experts" of the day—his central place in their
great story:

> *You study the Scriptures diligently because you*
> *think that in them you have eternal life. These*
> *are the very Scriptures that testify about me,*
> *yet you refuse to come to me to have life. . . . If*
> *you believed Moses, you would believe me, for*
> *he wrote about me (John 5:39–40, 46).*

Such claims were not typically well-received.

It has been said that if the New Testament
is Jesus Christ *revealed*, the Old Testament is
Jesus Christ *concealed*. That is exactly right. To
paraphrase the late theologian B. B. Warfield,
the Old Testament is like a room full of
treasures, but the room is dimly lit. It is filled
with prophets that predict him, patterns that
preview him, and promises that anticipate him.
A sweeping view of the Bible's topography from
30,000 feet, focused on Christ, would therefore
look something like this:

Old Testament: anticipation

Gospels: manifestation

Acts: proclamation

Epistles: explanation

Revelation: consummation

From beginning to end, your Bible is an epic story about Jesus.[1]

And why is Jesus so central, so ultimate, so unequaled in its pages and in hearts around the world? Because only he came to earth, truly God and truly man, and lived a perfect life; died an

> THE AUTHOR WHO DESIGNED US TO WORSHIP AND ENJOY HIM—AND WHOM WE HAVE OFFENDED BECAUSE OF OUR REBELLION—STEPPED INTO HIS OWN STORY TO SALVAGE IT.

atoning death; and rose to vanquish sin, Satan, darkness, and death. Jesus was everything Adam failed to be, everything Israel failed to be, and everything we have failed to be. He succeeded where we have not. The Author who designed us to worship and enjoy him—and whom we have offended because of our rebellion—stepped into his own story to salvage it.

Above all, the story is one of *rescue*—God becoming man to bring man back to God. Though each of us deserves separation from God forever because of sin, Jesus went to the cross in the place of sinners to pay their penalty. Jesus loves to forgive; that's why he came. And he loves to make new; that's why he is coming again. Simply turn to him in trust and you can know him not as your Judge, but as your Savior and Friend.

In the meantime, approach the Scriptures Christocentrically—with a view to how the Bible in its entirety centers on Christ, the one in whom all the promises of God are "Yes" and "Amen" (2 Cor. 1:20). If you're looking for a collection of morality tales, check out *Aesop's Fables*. Otherwise, crack open the greatest story of all time, the only story in which the central character loves us back.

But be careful. He might just change your life.

CONCLUSION:

SEEING GOD WITH YOUR EARS

I sometimes hear people quip that we shouldn't make *too* much of the Bible, lest we inadvertently make an idol of it. "We worship Father, Son, and Holy Spirit," the remark usually goes, "not Father, Son, and Holy Bible."

I get what they're saying. I even affirm the point.

But forgive me if I don't think the danger in our day is taking God's Word too seriously. If anything, I'm certain we undersell how Scripture speaks of itself.

So while we must indeed avoid "bibliolatry"—treasuring Scripture more than its Author—it is striking to note just how tightly Scripture connects God's words with God himself. Consider, for example, what the psalmist prays:

> *When I am afraid, I put my trust in you.*
>   *In God, whose word I praise.*
> *(Ps. 56:3–4)*

What is he praising? The Word of God.

In another place the author has the audacity to write:

> *I will lift up my hands toward your*
> *commandments, which I love,*
>   *and I will meditate on your statutes.*
> *(Ps. 119:48, ESV)*

To what is he lifting his hands? Again, the Word of God.

If I started yawning every time my wife talks, it wouldn't satisfy her to hear, "Oh sweetie, I don't care much about your words; I just care about *you!*" Likewise, the way we treat the words of God reveals what we really think and feel about him. Approaching your Bible well, therefore, is nothing less than an act of worship. You're walking on holy ground. "The Bible," writes Jen Wilkin, "is our burning bush."[1]

Until Jesus splits the skies in blazing glory and our faith becomes sight, we must live in the age of the ear as we await the age of the eye.[2] So "for now," Augustine said sixteen centuries ago, "treat the Scripture of God as the face of God. Melt in its presence."[3] And as Spurgeon put it, "To me the Bible is not God, but it is God's voice, and I do not hear it without awe."[4]

Your Bible is a bottomless treasure chest of beauty and wonder, strength and joy. May you approach it for the rest of your days as if that's true, because it is.

RECOMMENDED RESOURCES

To help you approach the Bible studiously, I recommend securing a study Bible, such as the *ESV Study Bible* (Crossway, 2008), the *NIV Zondervan Study Bible* (Zondervan, 2015), or the *ESV Story of Redemption Bible* (Crossway, 2018). Additionally, some helpful guidebooks for studying and interpreting Scripture include:

- Matthew S. Harmon's *Asking the Right Questions: A Practical Guide to Understanding and Applying the Bible* (Crossway, 2017)

- Jen Wilkin's *Women of the Word: How to Study the Bible with Both Our Hearts and Our Minds* (Crossway, 2014)

- Robert L. Plummer's *40 Questions About Interpreting the Bible* (Kregel, 2010)

And some books that give a good overview of the larger story of the Bible include:

- Vaughan Roberts's *God's Big Picture* (IVP, 2009)
- T. Desmond Alexander's *From Eden to the New Jerusalem* (Kregel, 2009)
- D. A. Carson's *The God Who Is There* (Baker Books, 2010)
- Glen Scrivener's *Long Story Short* (Christian Focus, 2018)

If you're a parent or caregiver, be sure to check out:

- David Helm's *The Big Picture Story Bible* (Crossway, 2004)
- Sally Lloyd-Jones's *The Jesus Storybook Bible* (ZonderKidz, 2007)
- Kevin DeYoung's *The Biggest Story* (Crossway, 2017)

NOTES

1. Approach Your Bible Prayerfully

1. See chapter 9 in *When I Don't Desire God: How to Fight for Joy* (Crossway, 2013), pp. 137–54.

2. Charles Spurgeon, *Lectures to My Students* (1869; reproduced by Zondervan, 1954), p. 43.

3. In *Precious Remedies against Satan's Devices* (1652; reproduced by Banner of Truth, 1968), the Puritan Thomas Brooks observes, "Whatever sin [your heart] is most prone to, *that* the Devil will help forward. . . . Satan loves to sail with the wind, and to suit men's temptations to their conditions and inclinations" (16). In other words, Brooks is saying, Satan

custom-designs his snares to capitalize on the particular tendencies he observes in you.

4. John Piper on Twitter, October 20, 2009: www.twitter.com/johnpiper/status/5027319857

5. David Foster Wallace, "This Is Water," commencement address at Kenyon College (2005). Available at http://bulletin-archive.kenyon.edu/x4280.html

2. Approach Your Bible Humbly

1. Of course, the very existence of the universe is also the result of God speaking. In the beginning God created the heavens and the earth—with words.

2. The quote in full reads: "Revelation is a divinely initiated activity, God's free communication by which he turns his personal privacy into a deliberate disclosure of his reality." Carl F. H. Henry, *God, Revelation, and Authority, Vol. 2: God Who Speaks and Shows, Fifteen Theses, Part 1* (1976; reproduced by Crossway, 1999), p. 8.

3. Approach Your Bible Desperately

[1.] Losing one's appetite after "nibbling [from] the table of the world" is a word picture drawn from John Piper's *A Hunger for God: Desiring God through Fasting and Prayer* (Crossway, 2013), pp. 18, 26.

4. Approach Your Bible Studiously

[1.] *Theology* is the study of God, and *doxology* is the worship of God.

5. Approach Your Bible Obediently

[1.] Though we tend to think of modern individualism as being opposed to community, author Jonathan Leeman insightfully observes that it's more fundamentally opposed to authority: "Individualism . . . is not rooted in being anti-community. Everyone loves the idea of community (except, maybe, the hermit). Rather, [individualism is rooted] in being anti-authority: I will gladly hang out with you, so long as you don't tell me who I have to be or what I have to do." Jonathan

Leeman, *Don't Fire Your Church Members: The Case for Congregationalism* (B&H Academic, 2016), p. vii.

[2.] I am indebted to Tim Keller for a similar version of this illustration. See *Every Good Endeavor: Connecting Your Work to God's Work* (Dutton, 2012), p. 39.

6. Approach Your Bible Joyfully

[1.] See John Piper's *The Pleasures of God: Meditations on God's Delight in Being God* (Multnomah, 2005).

[2.] For a helpful, and beautiful, discussion of this point, see Michael Reeves's *Delighting in the Trinity: An Introduction to the Christian Faith* (IVP Academic, 2012).

[3.] It's important to remember that the Bible didn't fall from the sky all at once. Rather, it's an unfolding story written over the course of centuries to specific people facing specific historical situations. Every single word was written by a particular person, at a particular time, in a particular place, for a particular reason.

7. Approach Your Bible Expectantly

1. See Betsy Childs Howard's excellent book *Seasons of Waiting: Walking by Faith When Dreams Are Delayed* (Crossway, 2016).

2. Martin Luther, *Martin Luther's Basic Theological Writings*, third edition, edited by T. F. Lull and W. R. Russell (Minneapolis, MN: Fortress Press, 2012), pp. 292–94.

8. Approach Your Bible Communally

1. See Collin Hansen's insightful book *Blind Spots: Becoming a Courageous, Compassionate, and Commissioned Church* (Crossway, 2015).

2. Jen Wilkin creatively makes this point in her article, "Beware the Instagram Bible." Available at www.thegospelcoalition.org/ article/beware-the-instagram-bible.

3. I have in mind various kinds of diversity— ethnic, racial, cultural, educational, political, socioeconomic, and so on. This range exists in the body of Christ, but we must seek it out. Labor to love those who don't remind

you of you. And don't just serve them or smile at them; learn from them. Believers from other backgrounds will greatly enrich your understanding and application of God's Word. Especially if you are in the majority culture, humbly seek out voices and perspectives different from your own, because it's highly possible that you've never considered them.

4. Despite slightly different emphases, "pastor" and "elder" are interchangeable words in Scripture, referring to the same office in the local church.

5. Thabiti Anyabwile on Twitter, September 14, 2014: www.twitter.com/thabitianyabwil/status/511197295174774785

6. Two useful American tools for finding a healthy church in your area are the 9Marks church search (www.9marks.org/church-search) and The Gospel Coalition church directory (www.thegospelcoalition.org/churches).

9. Approach Your Bible Christocentrically

[1.] I draw this rubric from Tommy Nelson, longtime pastor of Denton Bible Church in Denton, Texas. Additional passages that reflect on the Old Testament's role in anticipating Christ include John 1:45; 8:56; 12:16; 2 Corinthians 1:20; 1 Peter 1:10–12 (cf. Luke 10:24); Acts 13:27, 29; 28:23.

Conclusion: Seeing God with Your Ears

[1.] Jen Wilkin, *Women of the Word: How to Study the Bible with Both Our Hearts and Our Minds* (Crossway, 2014), p. 26.

[2.] I first heard this distinction between the "age of the ear" (this present age) and the "age of the eye" (the age to come) from Mark Dever, senior pastor of Capitol Hill Baptist Church in Washington, D.C., and founder of 9Marks.

[3.] Quoted in Robert Louis Wilkin's *The Spirit of Early Christian Thought* (Yale University Press, 2003), p. 50.

[4.] Charles Spurgeon, "The Word a Sword," a sermon preached at the Metropolitan Tabernacle in London on May 17, 1887.

"It's not complicated: if Glen Scrivener writes it, I read it."

—Matt Smethurst